Japanese

Japanese

LULU GRIMES

This is a Parragon Publishing Book
First published in 2006

Parragon Publishing
Queen Street House
4 Queen Street
Bath BA1 1HE, UK

Copyright © Parragon Books Ltd 2006

ISBN: 1-40546-329-5

Printed in China

Produced by the Bridgewater Book
Company Ltd

Photographer: David Jordan
Home Economist: Kate Moseley

Notes for the Reader:
This book uses imperial, metric, or US
cup measurements. Follow the same
units of measurement throughout; do
not mix imperial and metric. All spoon
measurements are level: teaspoons are
assumed to be 5 ml, and tablespoons are
assumed to be 15 ml. Unless otherwise
stated, milk is assumed to be whole, eggs
and individual vegetables are medium,
and pepper is freshly ground black pepper.

Recipes using raw or very lightly cooked
eggs, fish, meat or poultry should be
avoided by children, the elderly, pregnant
women, convalescents, and anyone
suffering from an illness, but please note
that eating raw or very lightly cooked foods
may pose a health risk to anyone. Although
sushi is traditionally made using both raw
and cooked fish, all of the recipes in this
book can be made with cooked fish. If you
are using raw fish, then ensure that it is
as fresh as possible, has been bought
from a reputable supplier selling sushi-
or sashimi-grade fish, and has been stored
at a low temperature in a refrigerator until
serving. Ensure that the fish is prepared
using clean utensils.

Pregnant women and breast-feeding
women are advised to avoid eating peanut
products.

contents

introduction

Japanese cuisine is one of the healthiest, most varied, and beautifully presented in the world. The diversity of its recipes reflects the fact that Japan is made up of over 1,000 islands, including the four main islands—Hokkaido, Honshu (the largest), Shikoku, and Kyushu. Agriculture has always been limited—besides miles of coastland, much of the inland areas are mountainous. Traditionally, the Japanese relied on the rich catch from the coastal waters as well as seaweed to supplement the rice and vegetables that they were able to grow.

Neighboring China has had a considerable influence on Japanese cuisine, introducing soybeans from which the Japanese made tofu, miso, and soy sauce; tea, which was incorporated into the tea ceremony; and noodles. The Chinese also gave Japan Buddhism, and consequently the society became semivegetarian for several centuries. Portuguese traders in the 16th century brought with them deep-frying techniques which were then refined by the Japanese to make tempura, among other things. The 19th century saw the reintroduction of meat into the diet as Western influences became stronger, but even today, meat is considered expensive and is eaten in moderation.

The main characteristics of Japanese cuisine are the freshness of the ingredients, their seasonality, and the way in which each dish is presented. These tenets are most important to the meals that accompany the tea ceremony, or cha-kaiseki, but are applied throughout Japanese cuisine. The use of hashi (chopsticks) dictates that many ingredients are cut into bite-size pieces. It is said that if food cannot be drunk from a bowl or eaten with chopsticks, then it is not Japanese.

Food is eaten in as natural a state as possible—dishes are not highly seasoned in order to allow the flavor of the main ingredients to shine through. Instead, flavorings, such as wasabi (Japanese horseradish), shichimi togarashi (a seven-spice mixture), and sansho (Japanese pepper), are often added in the form of condiments or in dipping sauces. The main flavors in Japanese cooking are provided by shoyu (Japanese soy sauce), dashi (a stock made with dried bonito and seaweed), sake and mirin (rice wines), rice vinegar (su), sugar (soto), and miso (fermented soybean paste). The most important ingredient is short-grain rice, which is eaten with every meal.

As well as the painstakingly precise recipes prepared for kaiseki ryori, a light meal originally served during tea ceremonies, and the type of food eaten at home, the Japanese have several types of their own cuisine to choose from when they eat out, as well as a host of foreign ones. The five main styles of cooking at home are agemono (deep-fried), mushimono (steamed), nabemono (one-pot), nimono (simmered), and yakimono (broiled). As Western influences creep in, cooking styles in Japan are evolving, and as well as most households using a microwave, baking is now very fashionable. Food eaten out ranges from the traditional noodles and noodle soups, sashimi and sushi, yakitori (food broiled on skewers), and the many small dishes served with drinks in izakaya, the Japanese equivalent of a pub, and robatayaki (grills), to Western-style hambaagaa (hamburgers), served without the bun but with grated daikon, and kariraisu, the Japanese version of curry and rice. The Japanese are spoilt for choice!

steamed rice with pickles

Put the rice in a strainer and rinse in cold water until the water is clear, then drain.

Put the rice and water in a pan or electric rice cooker and let soak for at least 30 minutes.

Cover the pan and bring to a boil, then reduce the heat to very low and cook for 20 minutes, without lifting the lid, until the water has been absorbed and the rice is cooked through. Remove from the heat and let it steam for 10-15 minutes before serving. If using a rice cooker, just switch it on, and at the end of cooking, let it steam before you open the lid. Serve with pickles.

SERVES 4

1 lb/450 g Japanese
 short-grain rice
2½ cups water
Japanese pickles,
 to serve

soups, snacks, and street food

The Japanese eat soup as an accompaniment to a meal rather than as an appetizer. Soups tend to be clear and clean-tasting, simply flavored with, for example, miso, and with a few decorative ingredients added, so that they can accompany a range of dishes. Corn Potage, however, is something of an anomaly, being neither clear nor particularly attractive, but it is one of the most popular Japanese soups and can even be found in package form in supermarkets. Noodle soups are regarded as snacks or light meals in themselves and are served at street stalls to be slurped up during hungry moments throughout the day and night.

On the streets of Japan, there are plenty of eating opportunities. Tiny curb-side stalls sell yakitori—food cooked on skewers—with each usually offering a variety of ingredients, ranging from chicken to gingko nuts. Establishments called *izakaya* serve food to accompany drinks. These bar snacks, called *o-tsumami*, range from Edamame (soybeans), which are eaten by using the teeth to pull the beans out of their fuzzy pods, to Gyoza (dumplings), Tempura (vegetables or fish dipped in batter and deep-fried) and Beef Tataki (beef steak that has been briefly seared on the outside). Beer is commonly drunk with food, usually at the beginning of the meal and served ice cold. Wine has now become popular, although sake (rice wine) is still served with the food it best accompanies—raw fish. In Japan, to drink without eating would be unthinkable!

miso soup

SERVES 4

4 cups water

2 tsp dashi granules

6 oz/175 g silken tofu,
    drained and cut into
    small cubes

4 shiitake mushrooms
    or white mushrooms,
    finely sliced

4 tbsp miso paste

2 scallions, chopped

Put the water in a large pan with the dashi granules and bring to a boil. Add the tofu and mushrooms, reduce the heat, and let simmer for 3 minutes.

Stir in the miso paste and let simmer gently, stirring, until it has dissolved.

Add the scallions and serve immediately. If you leave the soup, the miso will settle, so give the soup a thorough stir before serving to recombine.

MISO DOESN'T BENEFIT FROM OVERCOOKING OR BOILING: BOTH MAKE IT TASTE BITTER SO KEEP EVERYTHING AT A GENTLE SIMMER.

japanese clear soup

SERVES 4

4 cups well-flavored
chicken stock

½ cup mirin

1 tbsp shoyu (Japanese
soy sauce)

4 shiitake mushrooms,
finely sliced

1 small carrot, finely sliced

4 fresh chives, each folded
in half and tied in a knot

4 very thin lemon slices

Put the stock in a large pan and bring to a
boil. Stir in the mirin and soy sauce, reduce
the heat, and let simmer for 2 minutes.

Add the mushrooms and carrot and let
simmer for 2 minutes.

Ladle the soup into small bowls, float a
knotted chive and a lemon slice on top, and
serve hot.

IF YOU HAVE TIME, USE A MINIATURE
DECORATIVE CUTTER TO CUT THE CARROT
SLICES INTO ATTRACTIVE SHAPES.

corn potage

Put the stock in a large pan and bring to a boil. Add the corn kernels and cook for 5 minutes, or until tender.

Strain the stock over a bowl, reserving the stock, and transfer the corn to a blender or food processor. Process to a purée.

Return the stock to the pan. Press the corn purée through the strainer into the pan to remove any remaining solid pieces.

Bring to a boil, then stir in the sake and sugar. Add the cornstarch mixture and cook, stirring constantly, until thickened. Drizzle in the beaten egg white, stirring in a circular motion, then add the scallions.

Ladle the soup into small bowls and serve hot.

SERVES 4

4 cups chicken stock

$1\frac{1}{8}$ cups fresh or frozen
   corn kernels

1 tbsp sake

$\frac{1}{2}$ tsp sugar

1 tbsp cornstarch, blended
   with 2 tbsp cold water

1 egg white, lightly beaten

2 scallions, thinly sliced

YOU CAN ADD EXTRA FLAVORS TO CORN POTAGE IF YOU LIKE.
FOR EXAMPLE, STIR IN SOME COOKED CRABMEAT OR SHREDDED
COOKED CHICKEN ALONG WITH THE SCALLIONS.

sashimi

SERVES 2

1 fresh mackerel, cleaned
   and filleted
generous ⅓ cup Japanese
   rice vinegar
3 raw scallops, in their shells
5½ oz/150 g fresh (sushi-
   grade) tuna (*maguro*)
5½ oz/150 g fresh (sushi-
   grade) salmon (*sake*)

To garnish

shredded daikon
fresh chives
shiso (beefsteak) leaves

To serve

wasabi paste
shoyu (Japanese soy sauce)

Put the mackerel fillets and rice vinegar in a shallow, nonmetallic dish, cover with plastic wrap, and let marinate in the refrigerator for 1 hour.

Remove the mackerel from the marinade and pat dry with paper towels. Skin, then slice the flesh diagonally.

To remove the scallops from their shells, insert a short, strong knife between the shells and twist to prise apart. Using the knife, separate the scallops from their shells.

Separate any corals from the bodies and discard. Remove and discard the white frills and any black matter. Remove and discard the membrane around the edge of the scallops and slice each scallop horizontally in half.

Put the scallops in a heatproof dish and pour over boiling water to cover. Using a slotted spoon, remove immediately and pat dry with paper towels.

Shape the tuna and salmon into neat rectangles, then slice into smaller rectangular slices.

Arrange all the fish and scallops on the shredded daikon in a platter and garnish with fresh chives and shiso leaves. Add a mound of wasabi paste and serve with dipping dishes of shoyu.

THE FISH FOR SASHIMI NEEDS TO BE ABSOLUTELY FRESH, SO BUY IT FROM A REPUTABLE SOURCE. PURCHASE THE MACKEREL WHOLE AND GET IT CLEANED IN FRONT OF YOU, OR DO IT YOURSELF.

gyoza

MAKES 24

24 gyoza won ton skins

oil, for pan-frying

2 tbsp Japanese rice
vinegar

2 tbsp shoyu (Japanese
soy sauce)

Filling

$3^1/_2$ oz/100 g Napa cabbage,
finely shredded

2 scallions, minced

$^3/_4$ cup fresh ground pork

$^1/_2$-inch/1-cm piece fresh
gingerroot, finely grated

2 garlic cloves, crushed

1 tbsp shoyu (Japanese
soy sauce)

2 tsp mirin

pinch of white pepper

salt

To make the filling, mix all the ingredients together in a bowl. Season to taste with salt.

Lay a gyoza won ton skin flat on the palm of your hand and put 1 heaping teaspoon of the filling in the center. Brush a little water around the edges of the won ton skin. Fold the skin sides up to meet in a ridge along the center and press the edges together. Brush the curved edges of the skin with a little more water and make a series of little folds along the edges. Repeat with the remaining gyoza won ton skins and filling.

Heat a little oil in a lidded skillet and add as many gyoza as will fill the bottom of the skillet with just a little space in between. Cook for 2 minutes, or until the undersides are browned.

Add water to a depth of about $^1/_8$ inch/ 3 mm, cover the pan, and let simmer over low heat for 6 minutes, or until the skins are translucent and cooked. Uncover and increase the heat to bubble away any excess water. Remove and keep warm while you cook the remaining gyoza.

Put the vinegar in a small dipping dish, stir in the soy sauce, and add a splash of water. Serve the gyoza with the sauce for dipping.

GYOZA WON TON SKINS CAN BE BOUGHT FRESH
OR FROZEN FROM JAPANESE STORES. YOU COULD
ALSO USE CHINESE-STYLE DUMPLING SKINS.

kara-age chicken

Cut the chicken into large cubes and put in a bowl. Add the soy sauce, mirin, ginger, and garlic and turn the chicken to coat well. Cover with plastic wrap and let marinate in a cool place for 20 minutes.

Preheat a wok, then fill one-third full with oil, or use a deep-fryer. Heat the oil to 350–375°F/180–190°C, or until a cube of bread browns in 30 seconds.

Meanwhile, mix the potato starch with the salt in a bowl. Lift the chicken out of the marinade and shake off any excess. Drop it into the potato starch and coat well, then shake off any excess.

Add the chicken to the oil, in batches, and cook for 6 minutes, or until crisp and brown. Remove, drain on paper towels, and keep hot while you cook the remaining chicken.

Serve with lemon wedges.

SERVES 4

6 skinless, boneless
  chicken thighs, about
  3½ oz/100 g each
4 tbsp shoyu (Japanese
  soy sauce)
4 tbsp mirin
2 tsp finely grated fresh
  gingerroot
2 garlic cloves, crushed
oil, for deep-frying
½ cup potato starch or
  cornstarch
pinch of salt
lemon wedges, to serve

KARA-AGE MEANS DEEP-FRIED. THIS RECIPE
ALSO WORKS WELL WITH CUBES OF FISH.

tempura

SERVES 4

5½ oz/150 g package
   tempura mix
4 shiitake mushrooms
4 fresh asparagus spears
4 slices sweet potato
1 red bell pepper, seeded
   and cut into strips
4 onion slices, cut
   widthwise into rings
oil, for deep-frying

Dipping sauce

2 tsp mirin
1 tbsp shoyu (Japanese
   soy sauce)
pinch of dashi granules,
   dissolved in 2 tbsp
   boiling water

To make the dipping sauce, mix the
ingredients together in a small dipping dish.

Mix the tempura with water according to
the package instructions. Don't try to make
the batter smooth—it should be a little
lumpy. Drop the vegetables into the batter.

Preheat a wok, then fill two-thirds full
with oil, or use a deep-fryer. Heat the oil to
350–375°F/180–190°C, or until a cube of
bread browns in 30 seconds. Lift 2–3 pieces
of tempura out of the batter, add to the oil,
and cook for 2–3 minutes, or until the
batter is a light golden color. Remove,
drain on paper towels, and keep hot while
you cook the remaining tempura pieces.

Serve with the dipping sauce.

> DO NOT COOK MORE THAN TWO OR THREE PIECES OF TEMPURA
> AT A TIME, OTHERWISE THE OIL TEMPERATURE WILL DROP AND
> THE TEMPURA WILL BE SOGGY. YOU CAN ALSO USE ORDINARY
> POTATO IN PLACE OF THE SWEET POTATO.

beef tataki

SERVES 4

1 lb 2 oz/500 g piece
   tenderloin steak, the thick
   center part, if possible
1 tbsp vegetable oil
ground white pepper
   and salt

Marinade

4 tbsp shoyu (Japanese
   soy sauce)
2 tbsp Japanese rice
   vinegar
2 tbsp sake
1 garlic clove, crushed

To garnish

2 scallions
shiso leaves

To make the marinade, mix all the ingredients together in a nonmetallic bowl, cover with plastic wrap, and set aside.

Season the steak to taste with the pepper and a little salt. Heat the oil in a heavy-bottom skillet until it is very hot, and seal the beef for 2 minutes on each side.

Remove from the skillet and plunge into ice water for a few seconds. Remove and shake dry, add to the marinade, and turn to coat well. Cover with plastic wrap and let marinate in the refrigerator for at least 30 minutes.

Remove the beef from the marinade. Thinly slice, then arrange on a plate in a long row on the shiso leaves. Garnish with the scallions.

PLUNGING THE STEAK INTO ICE WATER PREVENTS IT COOKING ANY FURTHER.

edamame

SERVES 4

1 lb 2 oz/500 g frozen
   soybeans, in their pods
sea salt flakes

Bring a large pan of water to a boil. Add
the beans and cook for 3 minutes, or
until tender.

Drain well, sprinkle with salt flakes
to taste, and toss together. Serve warm
or cold.

**THIS IS THE JAPANESE SNACK
THAT GOES BEST WITH BEER.**

yakitori chicken

MAKES 6 SKEWERS

6 tbsp shoyu (Japanese
  soy sauce)

6 tbsp mirin

4 tbsp sake

2 tbsp superfine sugar

4 skinless, boneless chicken
  thighs or 2 chicken breasts,
  about 14 oz/400 g total
  weight, cut into 24 chunks

4 scallions, cut into
  18 short lengths

Soak 6 short wooden skewers in water for at least 20 minutes to prevent burning.

Meanwhile, put the soy sauce, mirin, sake, and sugar in a small pan and bring to a boil. Reduce the heat and let simmer for 1 minute, then remove from the heat and let cool. Separate out a little of the mixture for drizzling over the skewers.

Preheat the broiler to high. Thread 4 pieces of chicken and 3 pieces of scallion onto each skewer, then brush the skewers with the soy sauce mixture. Cook under the broiler for 4 minutes, then turn over and brush with more soy sauce mixture. Cook for an additional 4 minutes, or until the chicken is tender and cooked through.

Serve the skewers drizzled with the reserved soy sauce mixture.

MIRIN IS A JAPANESE RICE WINE USED FOR COOKING; IT ADDS A SWEETNESS TO DISHES.

rice and noodles

Rice is fundamental to the Japanese diet. It has been cultivated in the country for over 2,000 years and was even once used as currency. Japanese culture reflects the importance of rice in its language—the word for cooked rice, *gohan*, also means "meal" and the literal meaning of breakfast, *asagohan*, is "morning rice," while the word *sushi* means "rice flavoured with vinegar" (*su*).

Rice is eaten every day in Japan, for breakfast, as a main dish, and as a side dish with all other meals. *Domburi* are dishes where the rice is topped with a cooked ingredient, such as Katsudon. *Chazuke* are dishes using cooked rice, often leftovers, with added ingredients. The Japanese use short-grain rice, which forms small clumps once cooked, making it ideal for use in sushi. Most rice is white and polished (*hakumai*) rather than unpolished (*gemmai*), because it is considered to have a much superior flavor, although the health-conscious are now increasingly turning to unpolished rice.

The concept of noodles came to Japan via China and quickly became established in the diet. Soba, made with buckwheat, are regarded as the authentic Japanese noodles, because they have no equivalent in China, as are udon and somen, which are made from wheat flour. Ramen noodles, together with Yaki Soba (fried noodles), on the other hand, are viewed as Chinese noodles, because both originated in China. Ramen, however, are the most popular noodles, and packages and pots of instant ramen are widely consumed.

yaki soba

SERVES 2

14 oz/400 g ramen noodles

1 onion, finely sliced

1$\frac{1}{3}$ cups bean sprouts

1 red bell pepper, seeded
and finely shredded

1 boneless, skin-on cooked
chicken breast, about
5$\frac{1}{2}$ oz/150 g, cooked
and sliced

12 cooked shelled shrimp

1 tbsp oil

2 tbsp shoyu (Japanese
soy sauce)

$\frac{1}{2}$ tbsp mirin

1 tsp sesame oil

1 tsp roasted sesame seeds

2 scallions, finely sliced

Cook the noodles according to the package instructions, drain well, and tip into a bowl.

Mix the onion, bean sprouts, red bell pepper, chicken, and shrimp together in a separate bowl. Stir through the noodles.

Preheat a wok or large skillet over high heat. Add the oil and heat until very hot. Add the noodle mixture and stir-fry for 4 minutes, or until golden, then add the shoyu, mirin, and sesame oil and toss together.

Divide between 2 plates, sprinkle with the sesame seeds and scallions, and serve immediately.

RAMEN NOODLES CAN EITHER BE DRIED AND PACKAGED (INSTANT NOODLES), OR FRESH EGG NOODLES.

udon noodle stir-fry with fish cakes and ginger

SERVES 2

2 x 5½-oz/150-g packs
   ready-to-wok udon noodles

1 leek, shredded

1⅓ cups bean sprouts

8 shiitake mushrooms,
   finely sliced

2 pieces Japanese fish
   cake, sliced

12 raw shrimp, shelled and
   deveined

2 eggs, beaten

oil, for stir-frying

2 tbsp shoyu (Japanese
   soy sauce)

3 tbsp mirin

2 tbsp chopped fresh
   cilantro leaves

To serve

chili oil

sesame oil

2 scallions, finely sliced

2 tbsp shredded beni-shoga
   (red ginger)

Rinse the noodles under cold running water to remove any oil and tip into a bowl.

Add the leek, bean sprouts, mushrooms, fish cake, shrimp, and eggs to the noodles and mix well to combine.

Preheat a wok or large skillet over high heat. Add a little oil and heat until very hot. Add the noodle mixture and stir-fry until golden, and the shrimp have turned pink and are cooked through.

Add the soy sauce, mirin, and cilantro and toss together. Divide the noodles between 2 bowls, drizzle with the chili and sesame oils, and sprinkle over the scallions and beni-shoga. Serve immediately.

BENI-SHOGA IS AVAILABLE FROM JAPANESE AND ASIAN STORES: IT IS BRIGHT RED AND OFTEN COMES READY SHREDDED.

broiled salmon noodle soup

Put the salmon in a shallow dish. Mix the ingredients for the marinade together in a small bowl or pitcher and pour over the salmon. Turn the salmon in the marinade to coat well. Cover with plastic wrap and let marinate in the refrigerator for 2 hours.

Preheat the broiler to high. Heat a little oil in a skillet with a heatproof handle, add the salmon skin-side down and cook for 2 minutes, or until the skin is crisp.

Transfer the skillet to the broiler and cook the salmon for 5 minutes, or until just cooked through.

Meanwhile, cook the noodles according to the package instructions, then drain. Heat the stock in a pan.

Divide the noodles between 4 bowls, add some spinach to each, and pour over the hot stock. Top with a piece of salmon.

SERVES 4

4 skin-on salmon fillets,
  about 10½ oz/300 g
  total weight
oil, for pan-frying
9 oz/250 g ramen noodles
generous 6⅓ cups stock
2 handfuls of spinach
  leaves

Marinade
2 tbsp sake
2 tbsp mirin
4 tbsp plum sauce
4 tbsp miso paste

THIS SALMON DISH WORKS EQUALLY
WELL SERVED WITH RICE OR A SALAD.

somen noodles with shrimp

SERVES 2

16 raw shrimp, shelled and
   deveined
3 shiitake mushrooms,
   finely sliced
¼ white or green cabbage,
   shredded
1 carrot, shredded
2 bundles of somen noodles
6 shiso leaves, shredded

Dressing

4 tbsp oil
1 tbsp sesame seeds, toasted
½ cup Japanese
   rice vinegar
1 tbsp sugar
1 tbsp usukuchi shoyu
   (Japanese light soy sauce)
salt

To make the dressing, mix 3 tablespoons
of the oil and all the remaining dressing
ingredients together, with salt to taste, in
a nonmetallic bowl.

Preheat the wok or skillet over high heat.
Add the remaining oil and heat until very
hot. Add the shrimp and cook, tossing
occasionally, until they have turned pink.

Add the mushrooms and stir-fry for
1 minute, then add the cabbage and carrot
and toss together. Remove from the heat
and let cool.

Cook the noodles according to the
package instructions, then drain. Put in a
large bowl with the shrimp mixture. Add
the dressing and toss well. Sprinkle with
the shiso leaves and serve.

SHISO LEAVES ARE DARK PURPLE WITH A GREEN
TINGE AND A JAGGED EDGE; THEY ARE OFTEN SOLD
AS SHISO SPROUTS GROWING IN LITTLE CARTONS.

katsudon

SERVES 4

4 tbsp all-purpose flour

1 egg, lightly beaten

generous 2¼ cups Tonkatsu
   (*panko*) bread crumbs

4 pork chops,
   about 5½ oz/150 g each,
   bones removed

oil, for pan-frying

scant 2½ cups dashi stock

4 tbsp shoyu (Japanese
   soy sauce)

2 tbsp mirin

1 onion, sliced

4 eggs

1 lb 5 oz/600 g cooked
   Japanese short-grain rice

Put the flour, egg, and bread crumbs separately into 3 shallow bowls large enough to fit a pork chop. Roll a rolling pin over each chop to thin it a little.

Dip each chop first in the flour, then in the egg, and finally in the bread crumbs to coat. Cover with plastic wrap and let chill in the refrigerator for 10 minutes, then dip again in the egg and bread crumbs.

Preheat a wok over high heat. Add oil to a depth of about ¾ inch/2 cm and heat until very hot. Add the chops, one at a time, reduce the heat to medium, and cook for 4 minutes on each side, or until the pork is cooked through and the bread crumbs are golden. Remove and slice.

Meanwhile, put the stock, soy sauce, and mirin in a pan and bring to a simmer. Add the onion and let simmer for 5 minutes. Beat the eggs in a bowl, then pour over the onions in the stock. Cover and cook for 1 minute.

Divide the rice between 4 bowls. Lay the pork slices on top, then ladle some of the egg, onion, and stock over the pork and rice. Serve immediately.

> **YOU CAN ALSO SERVE THE PORK ON TOP OF A BOWL OF NOODLE SOUP.**

mushroom rice pot

Put the rice in a strainer and rinse in cold water until the water is clear, then drain.

Put the rice and water in a pan or electric rice cooker and let soak for at least 30 minutes.

Add the mushrooms, abura-age, soy sauce, and sake to the pan or rice cooker. Cover the pan and bring to a boil, then reduce the heat to very low and cook for 20 minutes, without lifting the lid, until the water has been absorbed and the rice is cooked through. If using a rice cooker, just switch it on.

SERVES 4

1 lb 2 oz/500 g Japanese
   short-grain rice

2½ cups water

1-2 matsutake mushrooms,
   shredded

2 shiitake mushrooms,
   shredded

1 block of abura-age (fried
   tofu), cut into thin strips

4 tbsp shoyu (Japanese
   soy sauce)

4 tbsp sake

**MATSUTAKE OR PINE MUSHROOMS ARE IN
SEASON IN THE FALL IN JAPAN, AND ARE
HIGHLY PRIZED.**

sushi rice

ENOUGH FOR 24
STANDARD-SIZED
SUSHI ROLLS

1¼ cups Japanese short-
grain rice

scant 1½ cups water

1 piece kombu (sun-dried
kelp, optional)

2 tbsp sushi rice seasoning

Put the rice in a strainer and rinse in cold water until the water is clear, then drain.

Put the rice in a pan with the water, and the kombu, if using, cover and bring to a boil as quickly as possible. Remove the kombu, then reduce the heat and simmer for 10 minutes. Turn off the heat and let stand for 15 minutes without lifting the lid.

Put the hot rice in a *sushi-oke* (large, very shallow bowl) and pour the sushi rice seasoning evenly over the surface of the rice. Use one hand to mix the seasoning into the rice with quick cutting strokes using a *shamoji* (spatula) and the other hand to fan the rice in order to cool it down as quickly as you can. Mix the seasoning in carefully to avoid breaking any of the grains.

Serve when the rice is shiny and at room temperature.

RICE IS THE MOST IMPORTANT INGREDIENT IN SUSHI. THERE ARE SEVERAL BRANDS OF SUSHI RICE ON THE MARKET. ALL ARE WHITE AND SHORT-GRAIN, AND MARKED SPECIFICALLY "SUSHI RICE." IF YOU CAN'T FIND SUSHI RICE, USE ANOTHER TYPE OF SHORT-GRAIN WHITE RICE INSTEAD.

crab, asparagus, and shiitake rolls with ponzu sauce

MAKES 24 PIECES

6 fresh asparagus spears

1 tbsp oil

6 shiitake mushrooms, sliced

1 quantity freshly cooked
   Sushi Rice

6 small sheets toasted nori

wasabi paste

6 crab sticks, split in half
   lengthwise

Ponzu sauce

3 tbsp mirin

2 tbsp Japanese rice
   vinegar

1 tbsp usukuchi shoyu
   (Japanese light soy sauce)

2 tbsp bonito flakes

4 tbsp lemon juice

Fill a skillet with water and heat until simmering. Add the asparagus and cook until tender when pierced with the tip of a knife. Drain, cut into 3½-inch/9-cm lengths, and let cool.

To make the sauce, put all the ingredients in a small pan and bring to a boil. Turn off the heat and let cool.

Meanwhile, heat the oil in a skillet and cook the mushrooms over medium heat for 5 minutes, or until completely soft.

Divide the rice into 6 equal portions. Put a sheet of nori, shiny-side down, on a sushi rolling mat with the longest end toward you. Using wet hands, spread 1 portion of the rice in an even layer on the nori, leaving ¾ inch/2 cm of nori visible at the end furthest away from you.

Spread a small amount of wasabi onto the rice at the end nearest to you. Top with an asparagus spear, then add 2 pieces of crab stick alongside. Add a line of mushroom slices.

Fold the mat over, starting at the end where the ingredients are and tucking in the end of the nori to start the roll. Keep rolling, lifting up the mat as you go and keeping the pressure even but gentle, until you have finished the roll. Moisten the top edge of the nori with water to seal the sushi roll closed.

Remove the roll from the mat and cut into 4 even-size pieces with a wet, very sharp knife. Arrange the rolls on a plate. Repeat with the remaining ingredients and serve with the sauce.

SHIITAKE MUSHROOMS CAN BE BOUGHT BOTH FRESH AND DRIED. IF YOU CAN'T FIND THE FRESH MUSHROOMS, THEN SOAK DRIED ONES IN BOILING WATER FOR 30 MINUTES, DRAIN, AND SQUEEZE DRY. YOU CAN NOW COOK THEM ACCORDING TO THE RECIPE.

scattered sushi with smoked mackerel

Cook the snow peas in a pan of boiling salted water for 1 minute. Drain and let cool.

Shred the daikon using the finest setting on a mandoline or a very sharp knife. If you are using a knife, cut the daikon into long, thin slices and cut each slice along its length as finely as you can.

Mix the rice with the lemon rind and juice.

Divide the rice between 4 wooden or ceramic bowls—they should be about 3/4 inch/2 cm full. Sprinkle the scallions over the top. Arrange the mackerel, cucumber, snow peas, and daikon on top of the rice. Garnish with pickled ginger, nori strips, and a small mound of wasabi.

SERVES 4

8 snow peas

2-inch/5-cm piece daikon

1 quantity freshly cooked
  Sushi Rice

finely grated rind and juice
  of 1 lemon

2 scallions, minced

2 smoked mackerel, skinned
  and cut into diagonal
  strips

1/2 cucumber, peeled and
  cut into slices

salt

To garnish

pickled ginger

strips of toasted nori

wasabi paste

DAIKON IS A LONG, WHITE RADISH THAT HAS A CRISP
WHITE FLESH AND A PEPPERY FLAVOR. IT GOES WELL
WITH FISH AND IS OFTEN USED AS A GARNISH.

sweet chili salmon hand rolls

MAKES 6 PIECES

1 skin-on salmon fillet,
  about 5½ oz/150 g

1 tbsp oil

3 large sheets of toasted
  nori, halved

¼ quantity freshly cooked
  Sushi Rice

2 scallions, halved
  and shredded

4 tbsp Japanese
  mayonnaise

2 tbsp sweet chili sauce

salt and pepper

thin cucumber sticks,
  to serve

Season the salmon with salt and pepper to taste. Heat the oil in a skillet until very hot, add the salmon skin-side down, and cook for 2 minutes, or until the skin is very crisp. Reduce the heat to medium and cook for an additional 2 minutes. Turn the salmon over and cook for an additional minute, or until it is cooked through. Remove from the skillet and let cool, then flake the salmon, keeping some pieces attached to the crispy skin.

Lay a piece of nori out on the counter and put some rice on the sheet. Spread the rice out evenly so that it takes up the bottom two-thirds of the sheet. Lay a sixth of the salmon, salmon skin, and scallion on the rice, then drizzle over a little mayonnaise and dot on a tiny amount of the sweet chili sauce. Roll the nori into a cone, folding the bottom corner in as you roll. You will have to paste the join together with a couple of crushed grains of rice. Repeat with the remaining ingredients.

Serve with thin cucumber sticks and the remaining sweet chili sauce.

SWEET CHILI SAUCE IS AVAILABLE IN MANY DIFFERENT BRANDS. THE BEST ARE THAI BRANDS, AVAILABLE FROM ASIAN STORES.

shrimp and avocado skewers

MAKES 6

1 quantity freshly cooked
   Sushi Rice

6 small sheets toasted nori

1 tbsp Japanese
   mayonnaise

1 tsp finely grated
   lemon rind

12 cooked jumbo shrimp,
   shelled and deveined

2 ripe avocados, peeled,
   pitted, and cut into strips

2-inch/5-cm piece of
   cucumber, peeled and cut
   into thin sticks

6 bamboo skewers

Divide the rice into 6 equal portions. Put a sheet of nori, shiny-side down, on a sushi rolling mat with the longest end toward you. Using wet hands, spread 1 portion of the rice in an even layer on the nori, leaving $^3/_4$ inch/2 cm of nori visible at the end furthest away from you. Don't squash the rice or make the layer too thick—you should be able to see the nori through the rice.

Mix the mayonnaise and lemon rind together in a small bowl and spread some onto the rice at the end nearest to you. Lay 2 shrimp end to end on top of the mayonnaise, then put a line of avocado alongside. Lay a line of cucumber next to the avocado.

Fold the mat over, starting at the end where the ingredients are and tucking in the end of the nori to start the roll. Keep rolling, lifting up the mat as you go and keeping the pressure even but gentle until you have finished the roll. Moisten the top

edge of the nori with water to seal the sushi roll closed. Don't worry if anything falls out of the sides—just push it back in. The edges may well look ragged, but don't worry.

Remove the roll from the mat and cut into 4 even-size pieces with a wet, very sharp knife. Lay the pieces on their side. Push each bamboo skewer through 4 pieces, making sure that they are at the end so that you can eat them easily.

NORI SHEETS ARE MADE FROM DRIED LAVER SEAWEED AND COME IN DIFFERENT SIZES. BUY THOSE THAT ARE MARKED "TOASTED" IF POSSIBLE. UNTOASTED SHEETS ARE NOT AS CRISP OR HIGHLY FLAVORED, BUT YOU CAN TOAST THEM BY PASSING THE NONSHINY SIDE OVER A NAKED FLAME. WHEN ROLLING THE SHEETS, ALWAYS PUT THEM SHINY-SIDE DOWN ON THE MAT.

home cooking

The type of recipes that the Japanese cook at home reflects the tools available to them in the average Japanese kitchen. Ovens are both a luxury and a recent addition to homes, so most dishes rely on using a broiler or stove, or an electric skillet, which is often used at the table, or electric hotchpotch. No home would be without a rice cooker.

Nabe (hotchpotch) dishes include Seafood Nabe and Shabu-Shabu, which are usually served as ingredients and each person at the table cooks their own meal in a central hotchpotch. Okonomiyaki, a cross between a crêpe and an omelet, is found both in special restaurants and is cooked at home, and again, each person cooks their own. *Okonomi* literally means "as you like." Teppanyaki—food cooked on a flat plate or stovetop grill pan—is popular in restaurants of the same name and can be cooked at home at the table.

Western-style food (*Yoshoku*) is also popular in Japan, and dishes like Sweet Roast Pork are becoming increasingly common. Traditionally, the Japanese do not eat dessert after a meal, but would eat a few pieces of fresh fruit instead. Now rather more Western desserts such as Green Tea Ice Cream are creeping into the Japanese diet. A typical Japanese meal consists of rice, some soup, a main dish such as Salt-Broiled Mackerel, a salad or vegetables, and some pickles. The Japanese join their palms together and say *"itadakimasu"* before a meal and *"gochisousama deshita"* after a meal, as a way of expressing thanks for the food.

teriyaki chicken

SERVES 4

2 tbsp shoyu (Japanese
  soy sauce)

2 tbsp sake

2 tbsp mirin

1 tsp superfine sugar

1 tsp grated fresh
  gingerroot

1 garlic clove, crushed

4 skinless, boneless chicken
  thighs or 4 chicken
  breasts, about 5½ oz/
  150 g each

1 tbsp oil

steamed rice, to serve

strips of cucumber,
  to garnish

Mix the soy sauce, sake, mirin, sugar, ginger, and garlic together in a bowl. Add the chicken and turn to coat well. Cover with plastic wrap and let marinate in the refrigerator for at least 30 minutes.

Heat the oil in a heavy-bottom skillet. Remove the chicken from the marinade, add to the skillet, and cook for 4 minutes. Turn over, brush with the marinade, and cook for an additional 4–6 minutes, or until the chicken is tender and the juices run clear when a skewer is inserted into the thickest part of the meat. Do not brush with the marinade again without cooking thoroughly.

Serve sliced on the diagonal on a bed of rice and garnished with strips of cucumber.

SAKE IS A TYPE OF FERMENTED RICE DRINK. LIKE
WINE, IT WILL NOT KEEP FOR LONG ONCE OPENED.

okonomiyaki

SERVES 4

4 large green cabbage
  leaves
generous 2 cups all-
  purpose flour
2 eggs, beaten
scant 1 cup water
selection of thinly sliced
  steak, skinless, boneless
  chicken breast, raw
  shrimp, shelled, deveined,
  and halved, and/or
  mushrooms, sliced, about
  $3\frac{1}{2}$ oz/100 g per person
oil, for pan-frying

To serve

katsuo-bushi (dried smoked
  bonito)
aonori (dried green
  seaweed)
brown okonomiyaki sauce
Japanese mayonnaise

Shred the cabbage leaves. Mix the flour, cabbage, eggs, and water together in a bowl. Add your chosen selection of ingredients and mix in.

Heat a little oil in a skillet and add 4 tablespoons of the mixture. Cook until the underside is set, then flip over and cook the other side. Remove from the skillet and keep warm while you cook the remaining mixture.

Serve with katsuo-bushi, aonori, okonomiyaki sauce, and mayonnaise.

BROWN OKONOMIYAKI SAUCE IS AVAILABLE FROM ASIAN AND JAPANESE SUPERMARKETS.

Put the kombu in a shallow pot set over a heat source (see Cook's Tip) and cover with the water. Gently bring to a boil, then remove the kombu just before it actually starts to boil. Keep the water at a gentle simmer.

Meanwhile, mix the sauce ingredients together in a small dipping bowl.

To eat, swish one of the main ingredients around in the hot water—just for a few seconds for the beef and Napa cabbage, and 1 minute for the mushrooms and tofu—then dip it in the sauce. Serve with steamed rice.

SERVES 4

2 slices kombu
  (sun-dried kelp)
4 cups cold water
1 lb 2 oz/500 g top sirloin
  steak, very thinly sliced
1 lb 2 oz/500 g mixed
  mushrooms, such as
  shiitake, enoki, shimeji,
  and shirataki
1 lb 2 oz/500 g Napa
  cabbage, torn into pieces
1 lb/450 g firm tofu, drained
  and cut into cubes
steamed rice, to serve

Dipping sauce

2 tbsp shoyu (Japanese
  soy sauce)
1 tbsp lemon juice

SHABU-SHABU MEANS "SWISH-SWISH"—THE ACTION YOU USE TO COOK A VERY THIN SLICE OF BEEF IN HOT WATER. TO PREPARE THIS DISH, YOU WILL NEED A SHABU-SHABU OR SUKIAYKI POT FOR USE ON THE TABLETOP, AVAILABLE FROM JAPANESE STORES AND SOME KITCHENWARE STORES, OR YOU COULD USE A LARGE FONDUE POT INSTEAD.

sweet roast pork

SERVES 4

1 lb 10 oz/750 g boneless
   pork side (belly), rind and
   most of the fat removed
1 garlic clove, crushed
1 tbsp vegetable oil
salt
fresh watercress, to garnish

Marinade

8 tbsp shoyu (Japanese
   soy sauce)
4 tbsp sake
5 tbsp mirin
3 tbsp brown sugar

Preheat the oven to 400°F/200°C.

Rub the pork with the garlic and salt to taste. Heat the oil in a large skillet and brown the pork all over.

Transfer the pork to a baking sheet and roast in the preheated oven for 1½ hours, or until the pork is tender.

Meanwhile, mix all the marinade ingredients together in a bowl. Rinse the pork in hot water and shake off any excess. Lay the pork in a dish and pour over the marinade. Cover with plastic wrap and let marinate in the refrigerator for at least 2 hours.

Remove from the marinade, thinly slice to serve, and garnish with fresh watercress.

SERVE THIS COLD, OR REHEAT IT THOROUGHLY IF YOU PREFER.
COOKED SPINACH, OR DICED CUCUMBER DRESSED IN SESAME
OIL, WOULD GO WELL WITH IT.

salt-broiled mackerel

SERVES 4

4 mackerel, cleaned and
  heads removed
4 tbsp sea salt flakes

Wash the mackerel, then pat dry with paper towels.

Put in a shallow dish and rub all over with the salt flakes. Cover with plastic wrap and leave in the refrigerator for about 30 minutes.

Preheat the broiler to high. Shake off any excess salt from the fish and cook under the broiler for 10–15 minutes until the fish is cooked through and the skin is crisp and browned.

Serve whole, or lift the flesh off the bone to serve.

SERVE THIS HIGHLY FLAVORED FISH WITH STEAMED RICE AND SOME SIMPLE GREEN VEGETABLES. YOU COULD USE MACKEREL FILLETS, BUT BE CAREFUL NOT TO SALT THE FLESH SIDE, BECAUSE THEY WILL END UP TOO SALTY.

steamed snapper

Preheat the oven to 350°F/180°C. Lay 4 pieces of parchment paper or foil on a baking sheet.

Sprinkle half the scallions and ginger in the center of the pieces of parchment paper and put the fish on top. Put some of the remaining scallions and ginger on top of the fish with half the sake. Sprinkle the remaining ingredients on top and season to taste with salt.

Fold the parchment paper into packages around the fillets. Bake in the preheated oven for 25–30 minutes, or until the fish feels firm through the parchment.

Serve onto individual plates at the table.

SERVES 4

4 scallions, shredded

4 thin slices fresh
  gingerroot, shredded

4 red snapper fillets

4 tbsp sake

2 tbsp mirin

2 tsp shoyu (Japanese
  soy sauce)

salt

THIS CAN BE MADE WITH 1 WHOLE RED SNAPPER,
CLEANED AND SCALED, IN WHICH CASE PREPARE
ON 1 LARGE PIECE OF PARCHMENT PAPER AND
PUT HALF THE SCALLIONS AND GINGER INSIDE
THE CAVITY OF THE FISH.

seafood nabe

SERVES 4

1 carrot, finely sliced

6 shiitake mushrooms, sliced

1 leek, finely sliced

8 oz/225 g skinless salmon
  fillet, cut into strips

12 raw shrimp, shelled and
  deveined

9 oz/250 g live mussels,
  scrubbed and debearded

8 scallops, shelled and
  cleaned

Stock

generous 6¹/₃ cups dashi
  stock

6 tbsp sake

4 tbsp mirin

1 tbsp shoyu (Japanese
  soy sauce)

To garnish

1¹/₂-inch/4-cm piece daikon

¹/₂ small fresh red chili

4 scallions, minced

1 lemon, cut into wedges

shoyu (Japanese soy sauce)

To prepare the garnishes, finely grate the daikon and chili together to make a pink paste. Shape it into a mound in a small serving dish. Put the scallions in a separate dish and the lemon wedges in another.

Put all the stock ingredients in a large fondue pot or ovenproof casserole and bring to a simmer. Add the vegetables and cook for 1 minute, then add some of the salmon and shrimp and cook for 1 minute. Add some of the shellfish and cook until the scallops have turned opaque and the mussels have opened. Discard any mussels that remain closed.

Serve with the garnishes. To eat, mix some shoyu with a squeeze of lemon and some scallion or daikon mixture. Lift the fish or shellfish out of the stock and dip in the sauce. Return the stock to the heat and add more ingredients as space becomes available in the pot.

THE EASIEST WAY TO MAKE DASHI STOCK IS TO USE SACHETS OF DASHI POWDER OR DASHI GRANULES. BOTH ARE READILY AVAILABLE FROM ASIAN STORES.

teppanyaki

SERVES 4

4 scallops, shelled and
cleaned, then sliced
horizontally in half

8 raw shrimp, shelled
and deveined

1 skinless salmon fillet,
about 5$\frac{1}{2}$ oz/150 g, cut
into strips

1 tenderloin steak, about
5$\frac{1}{2}$ oz/150 g, sliced

8 shiitake mushrooms,
a cross cut in the top
of each

1 red bell pepper, seeded
and cut into squares

oil, for grilling

Tare sauce

4 tbsp shoyu (Japanese
soy sauce)

2 tbsp mirin

1 garlic clove, crushed

Arrange the main ingredients on a plate.
Mix all the sauce ingredients together in
a dipping bowl.

Heat a teppan (see Cook's Tip) and add a
little oil. Cook the seafood, steak, mushrooms,
and bell pepper individually on the teppan,
adding a little more oil as necessary. Dip
the ingredients in the sauce as you eat them.

A TEPPAN IS A STOVETOP GRILL PAN. THESE ARE
AVAILABLE FROM MOST JAPANESE STORES.

green tea ice cream

Pour the milk into a pan and heat to boiling point. Meanwhile, whisk the egg yolks with the sugar in a heatproof bowl.

Pour the milk onto the egg mixture, stirring constantly, then pour all the mixture back into the pan and stir well.

Cook over low heat, stirring constantly, for 3 minutes, or until the mixture is thick enough to coat the back of a spoon. Remove from the heat and let cool.

Mix the green tea powder with the hot water in a pitcher, pour into the cooled custard, and mix well. Fold in the cream.

Transfer to an ice-cream maker and freeze according to the manufacturer's instructions. Alternatively, transfer to a freezerproof container and freeze for 2 hours. Turn into a bowl and beat with a fork to break down the ice crystals, then return to the freezerproof container and freeze for an additional 2 hours. Beat again, then return to the freezer and freeze overnight, or until solid.

SERVES 4

scant 1 cup milk

2 egg yolks

2 tbsp superfine sugar

2 tbsp maccha green
  tea powder

generous $\frac{1}{3}$ cup hot water

scant 1 cup heavy cream,
  lightly whipped

MACCHA TEA POWDER IS OFTEN SOLD AT HEALTH-FOOD STORES. TO MAKE IT INTO TEA, IT IS DISSOLVED IN HOT WATER AND WHISKED UNTIL IT HAS A LIGHT FROTH ON TOP.

litchi sherbet

SERVES 4

14 oz/400 g canned litchis
   or 1 lb/450 g fresh litchis,
   peeled and pitted
2 tbsp confectioners' sugar
1 egg white
1 lemon, thinly sliced,
   to decorate

Put the litchi flesh and sugar in a blender or food processor and process to a purée.

Press the litchi purée through a strainer to remove any remaining solid pieces, transfer to a freezerproof container, and freeze for 3 hours.

Turn the mixture into the blender or food processor and process until slushy. With the motor running, add the egg white, then return the mixture to the freezerproof container and freeze for 8 hours or overnight.

TO SERVE A LIGHT, FLUFFY SHERBET, RETURN THE MIXTURE TO A FOOD PROCESSOR AND WHIZZ JUST BEFORE SERVING, THEN SPOON INTO ICED CUPS OR BOWLS.

mango mold

SERVES 4

scant 2¹/₂ cups mango juice

1¹/₂ tbsp agar powder or
flakes

¹/₂ cup hot water

peanut oil, for brushing
(optional)

Put the mango juice in a heatproof bowl.

Put the agar in a pan with the water and bring to a simmer. Let simmer gently for 2–3 minutes, then pour into the fruit juice and mix well.

Brush a shallow, rectangular pan with oil, or line with plastic wrap. Pour in the mango mixture, cover with plastic wrap, and let chill for 4 hours, or until set.

Cut into cubes or diamond shapes to serve.

AGAR MELTS AT A HIGHER TEMPERATURE THAN GELATIN AND DOES NOT NEED TO BE KEPT AS COLD WHEN IT SETS.

vegetables, tofu, and egg

Japan was a largely Buddhist society for over a century, so vegetables were a main source of nutrition for many people. Many vegetables that we recognize in the West, such as pumpkin, sweet potatoes, and bell peppers, were brought into the country by the Portuguese in the 16th century, and tomatoes and asparagus arrived in another wave in the 19th century. Traditionally, the progression of the seasons, highlighted by the availability of certain fruit and vegetables, has been cherished, but this practice, as in other countries, is now in decline and most produce is available year-round. When vegetables were less easy to come by, seaweed (*kaiso*) was used as a substitute and as a result is common in the Japanese diet. Nori, wakame, and konbu are the most common varieties, the first being most often used in sheets for wrapping sushi or shredded for sprinkling over dishes, the second in miso soups, and the third to make dashi. All can be used as a vegetable in salads.

Tofu is a common ingredient in Japanese cuisine and a good source of protein. Although the Chinese character (*kanji*) ascribed to it means "rotten beans," it is actually made from soybean milk. There are several types: *kinugoshi-dofu* (silken tofu), used for Agedashi Tofu and also eaten cold with condiments, *momen-dofu* (cotton tofu), which is robust enough to fry, and *yaki-dofu* (broiled tofu), which is ready-fried. Another good source of protein are eggs, which appear as a main ingredient in omelets such as Datemaki as well as steamed dishes like Charwan Mushi. They are also used as toppings, stirred through soups, and marinated in miso.

agedashi dofu

SERVES 2

$^2/_3$ cup water

2 tsp dashi granules

2 tbsp shoyu (Japanese soy sauce)

2 tbsp mirin

vegetable oil, for deep-frying

10$^1/_2$ oz/300 g silken tofu, drained on paper towels and cut into 4 cubes

2 tbsp all-purpose flour

1 tsp grated fresh gingerroot

2 tsp grated daikon

$^1/_4$ tsp kezuri-bushi shavings

Put the water in a pan with the dashi granules and bring to a boil. Add the shoyu and mirin and cook for 1 minute. Keep warm.

Preheat a wok, then fill one-third full with oil, or use a deep-fryer. Heat the oil to 350–375°F/180–190°C, or until a cube of bread browns in 30 seconds. Meanwhile, dust the tofu cubes with the flour.

Add the tofu to the oil, in batches, and cook until lightly golden in color. Remove, drain on paper towels, and keep hot while you cook the remaining tofu cubes.

Put 2 pieces of tofu in each of 2 bowls and divide the dashi stock between them. Top with ginger, daikon, and kezuri-bushi.

KEZURI-BUSHI ARE DRIED BONITO SHAVINGS. YOU CAN BUY THEM AT JAPANESE STORES.

cold tofu with chili and scallion

SERVES 2

10½ oz/300 g silken tofu,
   drained
4 tbsp vegetable oil
2 scallions, finely sliced
½ fresh red chili,
   finely sliced
1 tbsp shoyu (Japanese
   soy sauce)
1 tsp sesame oil

Put the tofu on a heatproof plate and cut through the block into cubes, but keep the block intact.

Heat the oil in a small pan over high heat until hot. Add the scallions and chili and wait until they begin to sizzle.

Pour the hot oil mixture over the tofu, then sprinkle with the shoyu and sesame oil. Serve as a block.

LOOK FOR SILKEN TOFU FOR THIS RECIPE.
FIRMER TOFU WON'T GIVE YOU THE RIGHT
KIND OF TEXTURE COMBINATION.

eggplant with miso

Cut the eggplants into wedges.

Preheat a wok over high heat. Add a little oil and heat until very hot. Stir-fry the eggplant, in batches, for 4 minutes, or until browned and cooked through.

Return all the eggplant to the wok together with the chili and stir together. Add the remaining ingredients and toss everything together. Cook, stirring, until the sauce thickens.

Serve immediately.

SERVES 4

2 eggplants

oil, for stir-frying

1 fresh red chili, sliced

2 tbsp sake

4 tbsp mirin

2 tbsp shoyu (Japanese soy sauce)

3 tbsp hatcho miso

2 tbsp water

HATCHO MISO IS A DARK MISO THAT IS AGED FOR ABOUT TWO YEARS; IT HAS A DEEPER FLAVOR THAN LIGHTER MISO.

seaweed salad

SERVES 4

³/₄ oz/20 g assorted dried
   seaweed, such as wakame,
   hijiki, and arame

½ cucumber, halved
   lengthwise

2 scallions, shredded

1 box of mustard and cress

2 tbsp Japanese rice
   vinegar

2 tsp shoyu (Japanese
   soy sauce)

1 tbsp mirin

2 tsp sesame oil

1 tsp white miso

Soak the different seaweeds in separate bowls of cold water—the wakame will need 10 minutes and the others 30 minutes—then drain.

Cook the wakame only in a pan of boiling water for 2 minutes, then drain and let cool.

Put all the seaweeds in a bowl. Scoop the seeds out of the cucumber and finely slice the flesh. Add to the seaweeds with the scallions and mustard and cress.

Mix the remaining ingredients in a pitcher, add to the bowl, and toss together.

THERE ARE SEVERAL BRANDS OF MISO ON THE MARKET, MOSTLY WHITE AND RED VARIETIES. WHITE MISO HAS A MILDER FLAVOR.

green beans
with **sesame dressing**

SERVES 4

7 oz/200 g green beans

pinch of salt

1 tablespoon sesame paste

1 tsp superfine sugar

1 tsp miso paste

2 tsp shoyu (Japanese
   soy sauce)

Cook the beans in a pan of simmering water for 4–5 minutes, or until tender, then remove from the heat and drain.

Mix the remaining ingredients together to a spoonable paste in a bowl. Toss the beans in the paste, then let cool before serving.

THERE ARE TWO STYLES OF SESAME PASTE: MEDITERRANEAN-STYLE, CALLED TAHINI, IS MADE WITH UNROASTED SEEDS; ASIAN-STYLE IS MADE WITH ROASTED SEEDS. THE ROASTED PASTE IS MUCH STRONGER.

soy roast pumpkin

Preheat the oven to 400°F/200°C.

Peel the pumpkin, remove and discard the seeds, and cut the flesh into wedges.

Mix the soy sauce, oil, sake, and sesame seeds together in a bowl. Add the pumpkin pieces and toss to coat well.

Tip the pumpkin into a roasting pan and roast in the preheated oven for 20 minutes, or until tender and browned at the edges.

SERVES 4

½ pumpkin or 1 butternut
  squash
2 tbsp shoyu (Japanese
  soy sauce)
1 tbsp oil
1 tbsp sake
2 tbsp sesame seeds

**PUMPKIN IS VERY POPULAR IN JAPAN; IT IS
ALSO COMMONLY USED IN TEMPURA.**

charwan mushi

MAKES 4

1 tsp sesame oil

1 tbsp oil

4 shiitake mushrooms,
  finely sliced

3 fresh asparagus spears,
  cut into short lengths

3 eggs

$1/2$ tsp dashi granules

$1^1/_2$ tbsp mirin

1 tbsp shoyu (Japanese
  soy sauce)

scant 1 cup water

ground white pepper
  and salt

Heat the oils in a skillet and cook the mushrooms and asparagus over low heat, stirring frequently, for 2 minutes, or until the asparagus is tender. Season to taste with salt. Divide the vegetables between 4 ramekins or small bowls.

Put the remaining ingredients, with pepper to taste, then beat together lightly in a pitcher and divide among the ramekins. Put the ramekins in a steamer basket set over a pan of boiling water and steam for 10–15 minutes until the egg is just set. Serve hot or warm.

THESE STEAMED EGG CUSTARDS SHOULD BE SOFT RATHER THAN SET HARD. YOU COULD USE CUBES OF COOKED CHICKEN OR COOKED SHELLED SHRIMP INSTEAD OF THE VEGETABLES.

datemaki

SERVES 2

1 hanpen (soft fish cake),
   minced

generous ⅓ cup dashi stock

2 tbsp sugar

½ tbsp shoyu (Japanese
   soy sauce)

4 eggs, beaten

2 tsp oil

Mix all the ingredients, except the oil,
together in a bowl.

Preheat a rectangular Japanese omelet
pan or a large skillet over medium-high
heat. Heat the oil in the pan, pour in the
egg mixture, and cook until it is just set.
Slide the omelet onto a bamboo sushi
rolling mat.

Roll up the mat and press down slightly
to flatten off the top. Let cool completely.

Remove the omelet roll from the mat and
slice into 1¼-inch/3-cm lengths to serve.

**THIS SWEET ROLLED OMELET
IS TRADITIONALLY SERVED AT
JAPANESE NEW YEAR.**

index